1. Leveling up your craft to write a story that lives long after you've left the planet is what some might call a ridiculous goal.

2. You know that you will not tell that story after reading just one how-to-write book.

3. You know that you will not tell that story as the result of taking one seminar.

4. You know that creating a timeless work of art will require the dedication of a world-class athlete. You will be training your mind with as much ferocity and single-minded purpose as an Olympic gold medal hopeful. That kind of cognitive regimen excites you, but you just haven't found a convincing storytelling dojo to do that work.

5. The path to leveling up your creative craft is a dark and treacherous course. You've been at it a long time, and it often feels like you're wearing three-dimensional horse blinders. More times than you'd wish to admit, you're not sure if you are moving north or south or east or west. And the worst part? You can't see anyone else, anywhere going through what you're going through. You're all alone.

WELCOME TO THE STORY GRID UNIVERSE

HERE'S HOW WE CONTEND WITH THOSE TRUTHS

1. We believe we find meaning in the pursuit of creations that last longer than we do. This is *not* ridiculous. Seizing opportunities and overcoming obstacles as we stretch ourselves to reach for seemingly unreachable creations is transformational. We believe this pursuit is the most valuable and honorable way to spend our time here. Even if—especially if—we never reach our lofty creative goals.

2. Writing just one story isn't going to take us to the top. We're moving from point A to Point A^{5000}. We've got lots of mountains to climb, lots of rivers and oceans to cross, and many deep dark forests to traverse along the way. We need topographic guides, and if they're not available, we'll have to figure out how to write them ourselves.

3. We're drawn to seminars to consume the imparted wisdom of an icon in the arena, but we leave with something far more valuable than the curriculum. We get to meet the universe's other pilgrims and compare notes on the terrain.

4. The Story Grid Universe has a virtual Dojo, a university in which to work out and get stronger—a place to stumble, correct mistakes, and stumble again, until the moves become automatic and mesmerizing to outside observers.

5. The Story Grid Universe has a performance space, a publishing house dedicated to leveling up the craft with clear boundaries of progress, and the ancillary reference resources to pack for each project mission. There is an infinite number of paths to where you want to be, with a story that works. Seeing how others have made it down their own yellow-brick roads to release their creations into the timeless creative cosmos will help keep you on the straight and narrow path.

All are welcome—the more, the merrier. But please abide by the golden rule:

Put the work above all else, and trust the process.

THE FOUR CORE FRAMEWORK

NEEDS, LIFE VALUES, EMOTIONS, AND EVENTS IN STORYTELLING

SHAWN COYNE

STORY GRID

Story Grid Publishing LLC
223 Egremont Plain Road
PMB 191
Egremont, MA 01230

Cover Design by Magnus Rex
Edited by Leslie Watts and Shelly Sperry

First Story Grid Publishing Paperback Edition
May 2020

For Information about Special Discounts for Bulk
Purchases, please visit www.storygridpublishing.com

ISBN: 978-1-64501-016-6
Ebook: 978-1-64501-017-3

For

All Past, Present, and Future Story Nerds

ABOUT THIS BOOK

The best way to build a career as a writer is through word-of-mouth recommendations from people who love your work. If your words have excited, moved, or delighted people, they will pass on your stories to friends, and those friends will pass the stories on to *their* friends.

How do you inspire readers to feel so strongly about your work that they love and recommend it? You've got to satisfy the specific expectations they bring to the type, or *genre,* of your story. That means one of the most important questions any writer faces is: How do I know what my audience's expectations are? When you know the answer to that question, there's a follow-up: How do I make sure I can meet those expectations?

In *The Four Core Framework*, we locate the answers to both questions in stories' power to transform us—to open our hearts and our minds in myriad ways. As writers we provide moments of transformation, or catharsis, through four elements that together make up what Story Grid calls the Four Core Framework. By focusing on these elements—Core Need, Core Life Value, Core Emotion, and Core Event—this book will teach you how to emotionally connect with your audience and produce the catharsis they seek.

First let's nail down what we mean by *genre*.

[Please note that in the following pages "readers" encompasses any audience for your writing, including film, theater, and tv viewers as well as listeners who consume stories through audiobooks, songs, and around the kitchen table or campfire.]

1

CONTENT GENRES IN THE STORY GRID UNIVERSE

We see Story as a metaphysical phenomenon as expansive and explosive as our physical universe. Like the universe, Story is organized into patterns with specific structures and functions. Instead of constellations and galaxies, stories are organized into units called *content genres.* We can trace some of those content genres back to the very emergence of human cognition and creativity.

About two hundred thousand years ago, as our *Homo sapiens* ancestors' cognitive powers evolved, stories became integral to our survival. Naturally, the first stories concerned fundamental human needs: where to find food, how to build shelter, how to identify a mate, how to defend territory. We know about these early narratives because they are the stuff of our first cave paintings, sculptures, and other symbolic representations.

We think human communication gradually evolved from the simplest practical stories about physical survival into the primal content genre, Action Story. The War, Horror, and Crime genres probably followed as nomadic tribes learned to adapt to threats from others and supernatural forces they perceived working against them. Our ever-present Core Needs for physical survival and safety define these genres.

As human civilization grew more complex, so did our stories. We moved from small hunter-gatherer bands to larger, sedentary cultures cultivating the land and building cities. New story structures evolved to hold knowledge about how individuals fit into a group and how people conform to or rebel against others. The need to find meaningful ways to spend time on Earth and to chronicle how we relate to others produced more new story genres.

The bottom line is that content genres are categories, based on human needs, that divide the massive Story universe into twelve manageable constellations that we can observe and study. They are Action, War, Horror, Crime, Thriller, Western, Love, Performance, Society, Status, Morality and Worldview. For more information on all of the content genres, we recommend a deep dive into www.storygrid.com and a review of our genre-themed titles from Story Grid Publishing.

2

UNIFYING THREADS IN THE STORY GRID UNIVERSE

What if we want to view all kinds of stories through a unifying theory that shows us the boundaries of Story? What if we want a lens that helps us understand what Story is and does in our brains?

We're working on that.

As Story Grid methodology evolves, we apply new levels of resolution to our analysis of the structure and function of stories and gain new insights. One such insight has revealed that Worldview and Action are not only singular genres on their own but also form the boundaries of the universe of Story, encompassing all twelve genres.

This is what we see through our telescope at the moment, even as we reach for higher-resolution technologies all the time.

Every story poses a problem. The solution to that problem, revealed over the course of the story, is embedded in the story's universal takeaway or controlling idea. The protagonist or luminary agent tries to solve the problem presented by the inciting incident by relying on existing knowledge and practices designed to produce consistent results. This is the "on-the-ground" ***Action*** component of all stories.

When that knowledge and those practices break down as a result of a little ball of chaos we call the *phere* thrown into the narrative like a spanner in the works, the luminary agent must accept failure or transform their worldview. Such a transformation requires that they *break their cognitive frame.*

What do we mean by "breaking your cognitive frame"?

Breaking your frame goes beyond just "thinking outside the box" or seeing a problem from a new angle. Instead, the luminary agent must realize that the frame through which they interpret the world is not *capable* of seeing the solution to the particular problem they face. Using that awareness, they break, or dismantle, their current cognitive frame and assemble a new, more integrative one to replace it. This is the "in the clouds" ***Worldview*** component of all stories.

We believe the process of breaking and remaking our cognitive frames is the essence of Story, the way stories interact with our brains to produce knowledge and ultimately cultivate individual and collective wisdom.

Every story's controlling idea, or theme, communicates a lesson to readers who apply that knowledge to their own lives. That application breaks our frames and expands our ability to experience and conform to reality. As you read any story, no matter how simple or complex, you experience a shift from ignorance to knowledge linked to an emotional catharsis. Catharsis is the frame break, the insightful eureka moment that expands our cognitive framing. Readers crave that catharsis, and it helps us makes sense of our life experience.

And we read masterworks over and over again because, building upon the Four Core Framework, they strike at the heart of our most important problems as humans. They constantly break our framing, opening it up wider and wider, allowing us to make better sense of the world.

We'll have more to say about the boundaries and laws of the Story Grid universe in the work to come. For now, you need to know that breaking the cognitive frame is critical to delivering on your readers' expectations.

3

WHAT READERS WANT AND NEED

Every great story arises, at the atomic level, from a question about the human condition. *How do I save myself and others from death? How do I find and sustain a loving connection with another person? How do I achieve esteem and respect in my community?* These fundamental questions and others are answered in your story's *controlling idea or theme,* which is the bit of knowledge your readers are seeking when they choose a particular genre of story.

Story Grid can help you answer questions about reader expectations by bringing the *core* of your story into focus. The core makes a story irresistible, memorable, and worth sharing by providing readers with a cathartic emotional moment. We'll look at how each of the elements that make up the Four Core Framework supports the others and how they work together to determine whether readers walk away fully satisfied after turning the final page of your story.

The elements of our Four Core Framework are:

- The Core Need (survival or esteem, for example)
- The Core Life Values (a range from life to death or impotence to power, for example)
- The Core Emotion (excitement or admiration, for example)
- The Core Event (a scene demonstrating proof of love or a showdown between the protagonist and antagonist, for example)

When we're deep in a book that captivates us, we feel ourselves living through our favorite characters and experiencing strong emotions because of that connection. Let's look at how the Four Core Framework can help you create that experience and the ultimate goal of an emotional catharsis for your readers.

The Core Need is the first of our four essentials. Your protagonist's Core Need is the spinal cord of your story, often obscured by a lot of "wants" that are more obvious to readers at first. Put another way, the Core Need is an electric current of Truth that both the protagonist and antagonist spend a lot of time ignoring, hiding from, or running away from. This power source makes your book an all-night read. We sometimes say the Core Need is the subconscious *object of desire* shared by the protagonist and antagonist.

Your characters' success in fulfilling their Core Need creates a catharsis for your reader. It contributes, along with the Core Life Value and the Core Emotion, to defining your story's controlling idea or theme. The Core Need is most in jeopardy during the Core Event.

Core Needs are universal, shared by all humans. At Story Grid, we find psychologist Abraham Maslow's hierarchy of human needs to be a useful representation, and you'll find the Story Grid version—the Gas Gauge of Human Needs—at www.storygrid.com.

Core Needs include survival, safety, individual sovereignty, connection, esteem, recognition, self-actualization, and self-transcendence.

The Core Life Value is the next element of our Four Core Framework. Every story has a yardstick that measures where the characters' actions are along a spectrum or range of life values specific to that story. For example, an action story follows changes on a spectrum of *life to death*; a crime story, on a spectrum of *injustice to justice;* and a love story, on a spectrum of *hate to love.*

Deeply satisfying stories will include more than one Life Value spectrum because characters' actions will create change that is both internal and external in a variety of ways. But there will always be a Core Value that describes the primary, or global, change from the beginning to the end of the story. Like Core Needs, Core Values are universal, and they contribute to your story's controlling idea.

Core Life Values include spectrums from death to life, dishonor to honor, damnation to life, injustice to justice, subjugation to freedom, hate to love, shame to respect, impotence to power, failure to success, ignorance to wisdom, as well as selfishness to altruism.

The Core Emotion is the third of our four essentials. Your story should make readers *feel* something in order to become real and relevant. If a story doesn't inspire readers to feel that Core Emotion, it's just a sequence of events that won't make sense. If we don't feel anything, we cannot make sense of the characters' experiences, and we'll never be fully immersed in the story. Even if a story is occasionally compelling, perhaps because of spectacular action sequences or titillation, it will ultimately fall flat if it lacks an emotional catharsis built up scene by scene.

Core Emotions, of course, are also universal and contribute to your story's Controlling Idea. They include excitement, fear, intrigue, romance, excitement, triumph, admiration, satisfaction, pity, and contempt.

The Core Event, *our final element in the framework,* is the scene in which your story reaches the height of emotional tension built up in all the scenes that came before it. It answers the question raised by the inciting incident, and more importantly, it is the moment of payoff of the emotional catharsis. It's the moment of truth when your protagonist, whom we now call the *luminary agent,* must actualize insights gained from previous experiences. The Core Event integrates the other three core essentials as the luminary agent's Core Need defines the Core Life Value at stake, which elicits a Core Emotion response in the reader, listener, or viewer of the story. The Core Need is always in peril in the Core Event.

To put it bluntly, if you don't deliver fully on all the essentials in the Core Event, that's the moment your reader may throw the book across the room in frustration or walk out of the movie theater. And it's unlikely they'll be recommending your tales to friends at the coffee shop the next day.

Our overall expectations for any story—on

screen, in print, or even in conversation—meet an ultimate moment of truth in the Core Event. We show this in practical examples in the short story anthology, *Four Core Fiction* and Contender Guide that are companions to this book.

Let's now examine each of the twelve Story Grid content genres mentioned in the previous chapter and apply our Four Core essentials.

4

ACTION STORY

Core Need: Survival
Core Life Value: Death/Life
Core Emotion: Excitement
Core Event: Hero at the Mercy of the Villain

Action Story (or the Action genre) answers the complex question, "How do I overcome powerful external forces intent on killing other innocent victims and me?" As long as the human struggle to survive and pass on our genes to the next generation continues, action stories will fill our shelves, sell out theaters, and make our hearts race.

Action Story (or the Action genre) answers the complex question, "How do I overcome powerful external forces intent on killing other innocent victims and me?" As long as the human struggle to survive and pass on our genes to the next generation continues, action stories will fill our shelves, sell out theaters, and make our hearts race.

How do you deliver the experience Action Story readers are looking for?

The Core Need of action stories is our primal ***need to survive*** an inciting attack by a force of antagonism. The protagonist wants to defeat the antagonist and save others and themselves. The protagonist's deeper need, which all humans share, is to go beyond survival and make life and death meaningful. We must all find the courage to realize and activate our internal potential.

The Core Life Value of the Action genre derived from the need to survive spans ***life and death*** and all the subtle gradations in between. Damnation, or what we call the "negation of the negation" on the life-death spectrum, isn't usually in play in this genre, but the reader should understand what the fate worse than death would be for the major characters. The spectrum of life values includes the risk of an actual injury, illness, unconsciousness, and death.

Readers identify with the hero, whom we now call the *luminary agent*, and the *agency-deprived* victim in action stories. Readers often identify with the villain, or *shadow agent*, too.

When the luminary agent defeats the shadow agent, we feel the ***Core Emotion of excitement*** because if the luminary can successfully outwit or overpower an antagonist, perhaps we readers might too. Some of our first experiences with stories as young children inspire just such a feeling. The interactive action tale, *We're Going on a Bear Hunt* by Michael Rosen and Helen Oxenbury, is a perfect example.

Readers of action stories want to believe they can overcome their own shadow agents. If the characters we identify with can survive a plane crash in the Andes, take down aliens in the streets of New York, or defeat an undefeatable villain, surely we can overcome illness, injury, or a natural disaster. People do defeat villains in real life, practically every day, and we believe action stories play a great role in their forbearance.

When the global crisis of Action Story (usually the second crisis of the Middle Build) reaches the most extreme end of the life value spectrum, with death as a clear possibility, it sets up the ***Core Event.*** This crisis is also the moment when the luminary agent breaks their cognitive frame, seeking to make their death—if it must happen—meaningful.

Remember that the Core Event should integrate the other three core essentials as the luminary agent's Core Need defines the Core Life Value at stake, which elicits a Core Emotion response in the reader when attained. The Core Need is in peril as the luminary agent faces an impossible task and a great dilemma. Their choice depends on spontaneity rather than planning, which requires a cognitive shift as they attune their response to the changing environment. We call this Core Event the ***Hero at the Mercy of the Villain*** scene.

It's important to note that the excitement of Action Story reaches beyond the protagonist's external journey to a deeper universal human journey of self-actualization. When the luminary agent defeats the shadow agent to save the agency-deprived victim, they have expressed an inner gift, suggesting we readers can do the same. This affirmation of a greater meaning in our lives through a brush with death is why we read action stories. The controlling idea or theme of Action Story reflects this journey toward self-actualization, whether it is successful or not. *Meaningful life prevails when the luminary agent overpowers or outwits the villains, or death results when the protagonist fails to overpower or outwit the villains.*

By actualizing the potential of our unique gifts in an act of creation—actively expressing a newfound skill or insight through which we outwit or overpower the villain—creativity itself becomes the secret to defeating our external and internal antagonists.

Summing Up

In Action Stories, our own need to survive and find meaning in our lives allows us to identify with the luminary agent, and we respond to conflict on the life–death spectrum with excitement. In the Core Event, the Hero at the Mercy of the Villain scene, the Core Need to survive is most in jeopardy, the Life Value reaches the extreme of death, and the Core Emotion of excitement is at its height. By setting up and delivering this scene in a satisfying way, we meet the Action reader's expectations.

5

WAR STORY

Core Need: Safety
Core Life Value: Dishonor/Honor
Core Emotion: Intrigue
Core Event: The Big Battle

War Story answers the complex question, "How do we secure our group's survival while maintaining our humanity in the process?" War stories extend the Action genre's existential question to a larger group, adding more complexity and an emphasis on the *means* of survival, rather than just the end goal. Is the cause the characters are defending worth dying for? Readers of war stories experience intense emotions and powerful connections to the warriors—feeling pride in an honorable fight and shame or despair if they discover the cause is unworthy.

How do you deliver the experience War Story readers are looking for?

The *Core Need* for collective ***safety*** arises in the War genre when a force of antagonism attacks. These stories help us navigate our own battles to defend shared lives, homes, and beliefs.

Life and death stakes are in play, but the *Core Life Values* in war stories derive from the need for safety—one spans ***victory and defeat*** and the other, ***honor and dishonor.*** The most positive end of the value spectrum in a war story brings the characters victory with honor. The furthest extreme on the negative end brings victory with dishonor that is misrepresented as honorable.

We identify three subgenres in War Story, including the Pro-War Story, the Anti-War Story, and the Kinship of War Story. Each subgenre includes the victory–defeat range of values, but they also explore the values of honor and dishonor. Note that in the past we've used "brotherhood," a term of art in discussions of war stories, which historically feature all-male casts of characters. As we work toward less gendered language and in recognition that warriors are male, female, transgender, and nonbinary, we've replaced "brotherhood" with "kinship."

In war stories, readers see that victory is only meaningful when honor is maintained. Traditional war stories tell us that it is better to lose honorably, or even to lose dishonorably, than to win dishonorably. When we face a crisis in our ordinary lives that may require a more honorable or a less honorable choice, we remember this lesson. We also must consider whether the metaphorical battles of our ordinary lives are worth fighting as well as how we engage in them.

Readers identify with the luminary agents of war stories and the larger groups they defend. Just as in action stories, the risk of death for characters to whom we've become intimately connected evokes excitement and fear. But the ***Core Emotion in War Story is intrigue***, which we describe as an intense fascination about "what will happen next... how will the luminary agent/s contend with this seemingly impossible situation?"

The payoff of intrigue is the flavor of satisfaction when "the penny drops," that familiar feeling when we finally realize that two plus two equals four. In Steven Pressfield's *Gates of Fire*, for example, the warriors at the Battle of Thermopylae refuse to surrender and dishonor their community, despite facing certain slaughter. They explore and discover how to find a meaningful death as the means to save others from tyranny.

The global crisis of War Story usually brings us to the edges of each spectrum—victory-defeat and honor-dishonor—as the luminary agent must decide whether to express their gifts or face their own death and the group's destruction. The global crisis sets up the ***Core Event,*** which is the ***Big Battle*** scene. This crisis is also the moment when the luminary agent breaks their cognitive frame to examine whether the society and ideals they are fighting for are worthy of their death. The battle, which is both the global climax and the climax of the Ending Payoff, integrates all three core essentials as the luminary agent's Core Need defines the Core Life Value at stake, which when attained elicits a Core Emotion response in the reader. The Core Need is in peril and the luminary agent must choose between their own safety and the safety of the group.

The deeper takeaway of War Story lies in self-actualization through the expression of the gifts of love and self-sacrifice. Each character can become a hero by defending fellow warriors honorably in the face of horrific pain and loss. The existential question evolves into: "When is an individual death appropriate to enable the group to survive?" This affirmation of a greater meaning in our lives as members of a group is why we read war stories. The controlling idea or theme of War Story reflects a journey toward self-actualization. *War derives meaning from the noble love and self-sacrifice of warriors, and it lacks meaning when leaders corrupt warriors' sacrifices on the battlefield.*

Beyond the battlefield, the theme of leveling up each person's gifts of creativity and sharing them with others to solve problems is the purest expression of our humanity and what makes us far more powerful as a collective than as individuals. We will return to this theme in future books, particularly as we explore worldview stories.

Summing Up

In War Stories, our need for collective safety allows us to identify with the luminary agent and other characters, and we respond to conflicts on the victory-defeat and honor-dishonor spectrums with intrigue. In the Core Event, the Big Battle scene, the Core Need for safety is most in jeopardy, the Life Value reaches the extremes, and the Core Emotions are also at their highest. By setting up and delivering this scene in an innovative way, we deliver on the War Story reader's expectations.

6

HORROR STORY

Core Need: Safety
Core Life Value: Damnation/Life
Core Emotion: Fear
Core Event: Victim at the Mercy of the Monster

The Horror genre answers the complex question, "How do we secure and maintain the safety of our lives, our homes, and our beliefs when we are victimized by a manifestation of our deepest fears?" These stories conjure our worst nightmares, thus making the force of antagonism deeply personal to the protagonist, who may also be the victim. Like the boggart in J.K. Rowling's Harry Potter series, Horror Story's monsters are supernatural shapeshifters that give physical form to the protagonist's and victim's greatest fears.

How do you deliver the experience Horror Story readers are looking for?

The ***Core Need for safety*** arises when the monster—our greatest fears made manifest—attacks. The protagonist wants to defeat the monster to save others and themselves. Monsters, unlike the villains of action stories, cannot be reasoned with. Their essence is to devour the light. Think of Jack Torrance, a madman possessed by darkness, who attacks his wife and child in *The Shining*.

In Horror Story, the protagonist's deeper need, which all humans share, is to muster the courage to face not only the monster but fear in all its manifestations.

The ***Core Life Value*** of the Horror genre, derived from the need for safety, spans ***life and damnation*** and the gradations in between, including injury, illness, unconsciousness, and death. Damnation is a fate worse than death, which looms large and lurks around every dark corner in all horror stories. Damnation is always present when the victim is at the mercy of the monster, and at those moments, death seems like an act of mercy.

We see three subgenres of horror stories, based on the nature of the monster (ultimately, the nature of our fears), including the Uncanny, the Supernatural, and the

Ambiguous. Uncanny monsters are explainable and rational, supernatural monsters have a metaphysical explanation, and ambiguous monsters remain an unexplained mystery.

Before the luminary agent defeats the monster and survives, we feel the ***Core Emotion of fear***. Inspiring your reader to feel afraid, *truly afraid*, is challenging. Most of us rarely, if ever, face human, animal, or supernatural monsters. Instead, we are terrified of things that are more complicated than we think we can manage, including the loss of loved ones, terminal diseases, climate change, and financial disasters. Yet we usually manage to survive day by day, often by rehearsing stories about our fears in our minds and imagining better outcomes.

The global crisis of Horror Story brings us to the farthest reach of the life-damnation spectrum as the luminary agent must decide whether to express their gifts or face their own and/or the victim's death and damnation. The global crisis sets up the ***Core Event***, which is the ***Victim at the Mercy of the Monster*** scene, when the victim summons their inner hero and slays the monster or sacrifices themselves to preserve the lives of others. This scene, which is both the global climax and the climax of the Ending Payoff, integrates all three core essentials. The luminary agent's Core Need defines the Core Life Value at stake, which elicits a Core Emotion response in the reader. The Core Need is in peril and the luminary agent must face their fears or suffer damnation.

The universal takeaway of a horror story is the self-actualization of the protagonist through the expression of the gift of courage and selflessness in the face of fear. This affirmation of our ability to triumph over fear is why we read horror stories. The controlling idea or theme of Horror Story reflects this affirmation. *Life is preserved when the ordinary person overpowers or outwits a monster, facing the limits of human courage.*

Horror Story is Action Story intensified exponentially because the negative life value reaches into the darkest realms of the human psyche. In our ordinary lives we don't face ghouls or vampires, but we do face external and internal forces that threaten us with a fate worse than death. For example, damnation in our real lives would be causing the death or exploitation of someone we love and living with that truth for decades.

Summing Up

In Horror Stories, our need to feel safe allows us to identify with the luminary agent and the victim, and we respond to conflict on the life-damnation spectrum with fear. In the Core Event, the Victim at the Mercy of the Monster scene, the Core Need for safety is most in jeopardy, the Life Value of damnation is at the extreme, and the Core Emotion of fear reaches its height. By setting up and delivering this scene in an innovative way, you will deliver on the Horror Story reader's expectations.

7

CRIME STORY

Core Need: Safety
Core Life Value: Injustice/Justice
Core Emotion: Intrigue
Core Event: Exposure of the Criminal

Crime Story answers the complex question, "How do you expose defectors from society's conventions, laws, and codes and punish wrongdoing?" These stories follow characters who reject the social contract that holds society together. They pose compelling practical and philosophical questions for readers. How can we find and eliminate the bad apples in the system? What is the best way to punish a lawbreaker? What motivates a criminal? Will understanding those motivations help us improve the law or the judicial system?

How do you deliver the experience Crime Story readers are looking for?

The ***Core Need for safety*** arises when the inciting crime is discovered. Crime is an existential threat to the security and coherence of society, so the luminary agent must find the wrongdoers and bring them to justice. The star of every crime story, whether it involves a small-time heist or a grisly murder, is the intricate process by which the luminary agent solves this problem.

In Crime Story, the protagonist's deeper need, which all humans share, is to return order to a chaotic world, which often mirrors some inner psychological turmoil in the protagonist.

The ***Core Life Value*** of the Crime genre derived from the need for safety spans *justice and injustice* and the gradations beyond and in between, including tyranny and unfairness. The luminary agent acts on behalf of the larger society to pursue justice for agency-deprived victims.

There are at least a dozen subgenres within Crime Story, including many just within the category of murder mysteries. Rather than being based on fundamental life values as in war stories or the nature of the force of antagonism as in action and horror stories, the subgenre of crime stories often depend on the characteristics of the protagonist (a hardboiled detective, a police investigator), setting (a newsroom or courtroom drama), or type of crime (a heist caper or espionage).

When the luminary agent exposes the criminal, we feel the ***Core Emotion of intrigue***, which again we describe as a flavor of satisfaction when "the penny drops," that familiar feeling when things finally add up. Curiosity and the need to solve a puzzle drive readers to turn the pages of a crime story until the perpetrator is unmasked. If the criminal is never identified, the reader is fundamentally dissatisfied, but that doesn't mean the criminal always must be punished. In fact, it's common for wrongdoers to get away with their misdeeds in crime stories.

The global crisis of Crime Story brings us to the negative end of the justice-injustice spectrum as the luminary agent seems unable to discover the identity of the criminal and bring them to justice. The global crisis sets up the ***Core Event,*** which is the ***Exposure of the Criminal*** scene. The exposure of the criminal's identity, which is both the global climax and the climax of the Ending Payoff, integrates all three core essentials. The luminary agent's Core Need defines the Core Life Value at stake, which produces a Core Emotion response in the reader, resolving the feeling of intrigue. The Core Need for safety is in peril and the luminary agent often must choose between their own safety and the safety of the society or the victim for whom they seek justice.

The rise of the detective story, one of the most popular kinds of crime stories, parallels the growth of urbanization, industrialization, and bureaucracy. Millions of readers devour great detective stories in books, films, and tv series because modern life is fraught with complexity and the root causes of threats to our security are often a mystery. We take satisfaction when a Sherlock Holmes, Frank Columbo, or Jane Tennison exposes one clear source of trouble, whether it's an individual criminal or a corrupt organization. Real life doesn't always result in justice, so we can lose our sense of what right and wrong—or justice and tyranny—really mean. So when truth and justice prevail in a story, we feel a sense of security we crave.

The deeper takeaway of Crime Story lies in the courage to face the truth, no matter the consequences. The controlling idea or theme or a crime story touches on this: *Justice prevails when the protagonist overpowers or outwits the antagonist to reveal the truth.* Or, if the story ends with the escape of the criminal: *Tyranny prevails when the perpetrator overpowers or outwits the protagonist and the system.* Regardless of the outcome, knowing the meaning of justice in this situation, and who is to blame for injustice, gives us the cathartic release that is the point of the story.

With the Crime genre, the focus of Story's great conflicts moves further into conflicts between the individual and the group, as individual desires threaten society's integrity. Criminals believe the ends (getting exactly what they want as individuals) justify the means (breaking society's laws).

Summing Up

In Crime stories, our need to feel safe leads us to identify with the protagonist who seeks to uncover the perpetrator of the crime. We respond to conflict on the justice–injustice spectrum with a feeling of intrigue—a desire to see the puzzle solved. In the Core Event, the Exposing the Criminal scene, the Core Need for safety is most in jeopardy, the Life Value reaches the extreme of injustice, and the Core Emotion of intrigue is at its height just before the criminal is exposed. By setting up and delivering this scene in an innovative way, we meet the Crime Story reader's expectations.

8

THRILLER STORY

Core Need: Safety
Core Life Value: Damnation/Live
Core Emotion: Excitement
Core Event: Hero at the Mercy of the Villain

The Thriller genre answers the complex question, "How do we deal with ever-present and often incomprehensible forces of evil in everyday life?" Thriller stories blend elements of three other genres as the powerful individual protagonist (the heroic luminary agent) from the Action genre faces the embodiment of evil (the monster) from the Horror genre in a story about unmasking an antagonist who has committed a crime against society, as in the Crime genre. The luminary agent ends up as a victim and faces damnation if they fail to identify and defeat the shadow agent.

How do you deliver the experience Thriller Story readers are looking for?

The *Core Need* for ***safety*** arises in the Thriller genre when the antagonist or shadow agent commits an inciting crime indicative of a master villain. These stories include strong elements of psychological torment for the protagonist, which makes unleashing their gifts and solving the crime more difficult. The protagonist's worldview must shift to bring new insights before their gifts can emerge.

The *Core Life Value* spectrum derived from the need for safety ranges from ***life to damnation***. Damnation, or a fate worse than death, for the luminary agent is an ever-present threat. The crime committed by the antagonist becomes personal in some way for the protagonist, intensifying the relationship between the two and making their opposition even more exciting than in an Action or Crime story.

Like crime stories, thriller stories include at least a dozen genres based on setting and the type of crimes committed, including political thrillers, serial killer thrillers, and psychological thrillers.

When the luminary agent finally defeats the shadow agent, readers feel the ***Core Emotion of excitement***.

The controlling idea or theme of Thriller Story is: *Life is preserved when the protagonist succeeds in unleashing their unique gift, but death or damnation triumphs when they fail to do so.* In a dark and scary world of threats that attack our psyches as much as our physical bodies, Thrillers provide us with some hope that we can survive if we give the struggle with evil all our energy. In a thriller story, one of the villain's goals is to torment and destroy the protagonist, and one source of excitement for readers is in identifying the source of that deep antagonism. The power of the individual is often diminished in modern society, so the thriller story's focus on the power of an individual reminds us that we matter and our hidden gifts matter. As readers, we experience a cathartic release in the Thriller genre's affirmation of individual sovereignty as a defense against evil.

The global crisis of Thriller Story brings us to the negative end of the life–damnation spectrum as the luminary agent faces a dilemma about whether to express or withhold their gifts in the ***Core Event,*** which is the ***Hero at the Mercy of the Villain*** scene. This crisis forces the luminary agent to break their cognitive frame under the threat of a fate worse than death. This threat of damnation must be on the table. The Hero at the Mercy of the villain scene, which is both the global climax and the climax of the Ending Payoff, integrates all three core essentials. The luminary agent's Core Need for safety defines the Core Life Value of damnation at stake, which when attained, produces a Core Emotion response of excitement in the reader.

Similar to action stories, thrillers inspire us to identify with the protagonist, the victim, and often the villain as well. The enormous power divide between the protagonist and antagonist is similar to that in horror stories, but the fact that the force of evil is realistic, rather than supernatural, heightens the sense of fear for readers.

Summing Up

In Thriller stories, our need for safety leads us to identify with the protagonist who seeks to defeat an antagonist who personifies evil. We respond to the resolution of conflict on the life-damnation spectrum with excitement. In the Core Event, the Hero at the Mercy of the Villain scene, the Core Need for safety is most in jeopardy as the protagonist faces the extreme of damnation, or a fate worse than death. The Core Emotion of excitement is at its height during the confrontation between the luminary agent and the shadow agent. By setting up and delivering this scene in an innovative way, we meet the Thriller reader's expectations.

9

WESTERN STORY

Core Need: Individual Sovereignty
Core Life Value: Subjugation/Freedom
Core Emotion: Intrigue
Core Event: The Big Showdown

The Western Genre answers the complex question, "Is the autonomous, self-reliant individual in society dangerous to law and order or necessary to protect the powerless from tyranny?" Questions about the conflict between the individual and society, although present in other genres, reach their peak intensity in Western stories, in which individuals survive and thrive outside the conventional rules of society.

These tales combine elements of the Action, Crime, and Society genres with protagonists who often are both exalted and condemned.

How do you deliver the experience Western Story readers are looking for?

The *Core Need for individual sovereignty* arises from an inciting attack in which an antagonist (human, animal, or environmental) threatens the peace so much that the protagonist must risk subjugation or control by the larger society to restore order.

Although the classic Western story is set on the frontier of North America in the late nineteenth or early twentieth century, any frontier-like setting where law and order are not well established and individuals can free themselves from traditional social constraints can host a Western. For example, the science fiction television series *Firefly* followed the classic story of a stranger coming to town and helping maintain justice. It took place in outer space centuries in the future but still provided the experience fans of Westerns were looking for.

In a Western story, the protagonist's deeper need, which most humans share, is to transcend their own self-interest to offer their gift unconditionally, sacrificing themselves to help others.

The *Core Life Value* of the Western, derived from the need for individual sovereignty, spans subjugation and freedom. The luminary agent acts on behalf of the larger society to bring order from chaos but struggles not to surrender their freedom in the process.

We see three large subgenres within the Western genre based on how willing the protagonist is to give up some autonomy and serve society's need for order. In the vengeance Western, an outsider disrupts society to right a wrong. In the transition Western, the protagonist starts out as a well-integrated member of the society but is exiled and self-reliant by the end; and in the professional Western, the protagonist starts and ends the story acting outside the law.

In a Western story, when the luminary agent enters into conflict with the shadow agent, and through their sacrifice saves the agency-deprived victim, we feel excitement and fear. But the ***Core Emotion*** is ***intrigue*** because attaining the Core Life Value is a penny-drop revelation that sets the world right. In a Western, the villain is rarely torturing the protagonist on purpose, as in a thriller. Usually, the protagonist is simply getting in the way of the antagonist's goal.

The global crisis of Western Story brings us to the extreme of the subjugation-freedom spectrum as the luminary agent confronts a terrible choice, deciding whether to sacrifice their autonomy and subjugate themselves to the needs of the community in order to save the agency-deprived victim. The global crisis sets up the ***Core Event***, or the ***Big Showdown*** scene. The big showdown, which is both the global climax and the climax of the Ending Payoff, integrates all three core essentials. The protagonist's Core Need for individual sovereignty defines the Core Life Value at stake, which when attained evokes the Core Emotion of intrigue in the reader.

The universal takeaway of a Western story lies in self-sacrifice for the good of others. The controlling idea or theme of the Western genre is: *Justice prevails when an uncompromising individual sacrifices for the good of others, but tyranny reigns if the individual is betrayed by those they defend.* In either case, witnessing the protagonist—who values individual sovereignty above almost everything else—sacrifice for the good of others provides the cathartic release that is the point of the story.

Western stories mirror a struggle within all of us between our urge for freedom and our sustaining ties to the rule-bound society we live in. They remind us that rules matter, even when the world around us appears to be in chaos. And Westerns also externalize the commitments to morality and justice that we say we hold dear but that are rarely tested in ordinary life.

Summing Up

In Westerns, our need for individual sovereignty within a larger community leads us to identify with the protagonist who suffers the same conflict. We respond to the resolution of conflict on the subjugation-freedom spectrum with intrigue. In the Core Event, the Big Showdown scene, the Core Need for individual sovereignty is most in jeopardy as the protagonist faces the extreme Life Values of subjugation and death. The Core Emotion is at its height during the confrontation between the luminary agent and the shadow agent. By setting up and delivering this scene in an innovative way, you meet the Western genre reader's expectations.

10

LOVE STORY

Core Need: Connection
Core Life Value: Hate/Love
Core Emotion: Romance
Core Event: Proof of Love

Love Story answers the complex questions, "How do we navigate the emotional minefield that is love? How can we attract a mate, avoid heartbreak, and maintain a lasting relationship through a lifetime?" We agree with C.S. Lewis, who identified four flavors of love, including familial, friendship, romantic, and divine. Romantic love dominates the Love genre in literature.

There are too many definitions of "romance" to count, but we use a Story Grid-specific one here to describe the Core Emotion. It's a feeling akin to intrigue, a sense that the connections are falling into place as they should be. Whether one plus one equals two, or two minus one equals one.

How do you deliver the experience Love Story readers are looking for?

The ***Core Need for connection*** awakens in the inciting Lovers Meet scene of a love story. Romantic love is a need that's both external to our psyches—in that survival requires reproduction—and internal. We all yearn for connection, intimacy, and the assurance that another human being sees and knows us. Romantic love, or *eros*, requires more vulnerability, more risk, and a broader commitment than other relationships. Eros includes sexual desire but also asks that we grow and become better versions of ourselves so we can form a tighter bond with our beloved.

The ***Core Life Value*** of the Love genre derived from the need for connection spans ***love and hate*** and gradations in between and beyond. The negative points on the spectrum go beyond hate to indifference and hate that masquerades as love, and the positive aspects of love branch in three directions, depending on the subgenre of the love story. We see three subgenres of Love Story: obsession, which is driven by desire; courtship, which is driven by a need for commitment; and marriage, which is driven by a need for emotional intimacy.

When the lovers sacrifice selflessly, without hope that it will do them any good, we feel the ***Core Emotion of romance***, completing their connection as it should be. If the protagonists can find authentic connection, perhaps we can too. Love stories allow readers to *feel* romance without risk.

The moral weight of love stories is whatever requires the lovers to shift their Worldviews in a way that elevates them morally to find authentic love.

The positive universal takeaway, or controlling idea, of the Love genre is: *Love triumphs when lovers overcome moral failings and sacrifice their own needs for the fulfillment of the other.* And if the story offers an unhappy outcome: *Love fails when lovers don't evolve beyond shallow desire.* We can experience love and a sense of belonging if we are willing to risk being vulnerable, just like the characters we live through vicariously.

Love stories show us that love is possible and matters because it makes us better people. Unless it's a cautionary tale. Then they show us it's crucial to evolve past shallow, intoxicating pleasures, or we risk ruining ourselves for selfish ephemeral physical desires.

The global crisis of Love Story brings us to

the extreme edge of the hate-love spectrum as one lover must decide whether to overcome moral failings and make a sacrifice for the other lover without the promise of any benefit to themselves. The risk of losing love and connection must be on the table. The global crisis sparks the ***Core Event,*** which is the ***Proof of Love*** scene. The Proof of Love scene, which is both the global climax and the climax of the Ending Payoff, integrates all three core essentials. The luminary agent's Core Need for connection defines the Core Life Value of love at stake, which, when attained evokes a Core Emotion response in the reader. The Core Need of connection is in peril and so is the lovers' future happiness.

The Proof of Love is the most powerful moment in a love story because it's when readers feel the love for themselves. It proves the power of two together is exponentially stronger than the power of one. Imagine what those two lovers would do for their children if capable of such sacrifice for each other?

Summing Up

In Love Story, our need for connection in a variety of forms, including desire, commitment, and intimacy, allows us to identify with the lovers as protagonists, and we respond to the fulfillment of the couple's fate on the hate-love spectrum with a feeling of romance. In the Core Event, the Proof of Love scene, the Core Need for connection is most in evidence, the Life Value reaches an extreme, and the feeling of romance reaches its height. By setting up and delivering this scene in an innovative way, you meet the Love Story reader's expectations.

11

PERFORMANCE STORY

Core Need: Esteem
Core Life Value: Shame/Respect
Core Emotion: Triumph
Core Event: The Big Performance

Performance Story answers the complex question, "Will we do what is necessary to pursue and fully express our unique gifts, despite physical, psychological, or emotional difficulties?" These stories are about the outward expression of our internal gifts and our need for approval. Each person in the world has extraordinary inner gifts, but not everyone is willing to do what it takes to express them. Writers understand—perhaps better than most people—that growing and actualizing our potential takes great effort to attain skills through diligent work and level up our capacities by applying those skills day after day.

How do you deliver the experience Performance Story readers are looking for?

The ***Core Need for esteem*** arises from the inciting performance opportunity. We all have a deep desire to connect to people and groups that can help us in our life journeys, but we also want to be singled out as *unique and gifted* beings—people others identify as icons of success or value—and that's what performance opportunities such as scoring the goal in the big game or playing a perfect solo in the concert offer.

The luminary agent pursues mastery in their art, sport, or profession for positive recognition on one or more levels—intrapersonal (self), interpersonal (close relationships), and extrapersonal (third party). The actions we take to gain positive regard for one level won't necessarily gain us positive regard at another level. It's similar to the way you can find a service that is good, cheap, or fast, and you might meet two of those constraints, but you're never guaranteed all three.

The ***Core Life Value*** of the Performance genre derived from the need for esteem spans

shame and respect, and gradations in between. Performance stories show us that the full expression of our unique gifts, when uncoupled from personal shame and not *dependent* on respect from others, is the key to personal fulfillment.

There are four popular subgenres within the Performance genre, all of which are favorites among readers and especially filmgoers. We all love an exciting pressure-cooker moment that offers someone a singular moment to shine. Performance subgenres include sports stories, such as *Rocky*; visual arts stories such as *Mr. Turner;* music and dance stories, such as *Whiplash* and *Billy Elliot;* and business stories, such as *Big Night.*

When the luminary agent expresses their gift unconditionally and attains the Core Life Value of respect, we feel the ***Core Emotion of triumph.*** When we follow fictional characters or real people who express their gifts unconditionally by choosing to be vulnerable, we believe we may succeed despite our own vulnerabilities.

The global crisis of Performance Story brings us to an extreme edge of the shame-respect spectrum as the luminary agent faces a dilemma about whether to withhold or express their gifts unconditionally in the Core Event, which is the Big Performance scene. The risk of shame must be clearly at hand. The Big Performance scene, which is both the global climax and the climax of the Ending Payoff, integrates all three core essentials. The luminary agent's Core Need for esteem defines the Core Life Value at stake, which when attained produces the Core Emotion response of triumph.

The Big Performance always includes an audience that embodies everyone the luminary wants to please most. Will the boxer be able to handle the pressure? Will the young dancer choose to express their special gift at the risk of losing family and friends? Will the chef persist in the face of economic adversity? These questions grip the audience as the characters' actions reveal the answers.

The universal takeaway or controlling idea of a Performance story is: *We gain respect when we commit to expressing our gifts unconditionally. But shame results when we hold our gifts back for fear of criticism and/or reprisal.*

In the end, it's not how well the luminary "star" of the story does in the performance but the fact they are willing to take the risk.

Summing Up

In performance stories, our need for esteem from the group allows us to identify with the protagonist who wants to express their gifts under pressure. We respond to conflict on the shame-respect spectrum with a feeling of triumph when the luminary expresses their gifts unconditionally in the Core Event of the Big Performance. During this event, the Core Need for esteem is most in jeopardy, and the Core Emotion of triumph reaches its height when the protagonist attains the Life Value of respect. By setting up and delivering this scene in an innovative way, you meet the Performance reader's expectations.

12

SOCIETY STORY

Core Need: Recognition
Core Life Value: Impotence/Power
Core Emotion: Intrigue
Core Event: Revolution

Society Story answers the complex question, "What do we do in the face of tyranny? Do we stand against it or comply?" Society stories are about hierarchies of power between and within groups and the role of the individual in the group. These stories can take place in any setting—a school, a family, a workplace, or an entire society—as long as a disenfranchised group confronts a much more powerful ruling group. Society stories are inherently about groups, and yet the individual's ability to shape the group—for good or for ill—is usually a critical component in the events.

How do you deliver the experience Society Story readers are looking for?

The *Core Need* for ***recognition*** awakens in members of the disenfranchised class as a result of the inciting incident, a threat to the power hierarchy. This threat usually comes in the form of a crime or a speech by a visionary. A group that has been silenced and oppressed (the disenfranchised or agency-deprived) tries to seize agency to topple the controlling group (the tyrant or shadow agent). In some cases, the story will focus on an individual who stands in as a representative of an oppressed group—one woman who represents all disenfranchised women, for example.

The Society genre includes at least five subgenres based on the setting and type of disenfranchised group, including domestic or family stories, women's stories, biographical stories that use a single life to tell the story of a revolution, historical stories, and political stories.

The *Core Life Values* in society stories derive from the need for recognition and span a spectrum that includes ***impotence*** and ***power***. The brand of power at stake in a society story can be defined by other needs in addition to the Core Need, including justice, freedom, love, social mobility, or self-actualization.

Society Story's ***Core Emotions*** are as complex as the plots. When the Revolution succeeds or fails because the leaders of the disenfranchised class exposed the tyrant's lies or were co-opted, readers feel the ***Core Emotion*** of ***intrigue***. If the disenfranchised class defeats the shadow agent-tyrant, we might feel ***triumph***, perhaps because if the luminary agent can successfully lead a revolution by expressing their gift and regaining recognition, we might do the same. If luminary agents fail to express their gifts and are co-opted by the shadow agent, we will feel ***righteous indignation***. Through well-told society stories that end in co-option of the revolution's leaders, readers come to understand that we can all quickly transform into that which we seek to destroy.

The global crisis of Society Story brings us to the extreme of the power-impotence spectrum as the luminary agent confronts a choice. The luminary must decide whether to sacrifice themselves to expose the hypocrisy of the shadow agent. That decision comes to fruition in the ***Core Event***, or the ***Revolution*** scene. The revolution, which is both the global climax and the climax of the Ending Payoff, integrates all three core essentials. The protagonist's Core Need for recognition defines the Core Life Value of power at stake, which if not attained evokes the Core Emotion of righteous indignation in the reader and if achieved evokes triumph.

Often in society stories, the disenfranchised seize power only to have it taken away in the end, either violently or through the intellectual machinery of propaganda. The revolutionaries can be undermined through their own narratives as much as through outside forces.

People choose Society stories to experience the fear and exhilaration of rebelling against "the system" without real risk. The positive universal takeaway or controlling idea of a Society story is: *We gain power when we expose the hypocrisy of tyrants.* In contrast, the cautionary or negative controlling idea says that: *Tyrants can beat back revolutions by co-opting the leaders of the underclass.*

The Revolution scene is when the luminaries' gifts are expressed and power changes hands—a distinct shift in control from one segment of society to another. The revolution often includes a demonstration of physical force but can also be more peaceful. The only requirement of the revolution scene is that it must include a *revelation of truth.* A revelation about the true nature of the tyrant, exposing their lies and hypocrisy, is usually the catalyst for a successful revolution as in the film *Toy Story 3*. In other cases, the hypocrisy of a member of the revolutionary class is revealed, and the revolution fails, as in George Orwell's novel, *Animal Farm*. In that case, we come full circle, and power once again resides with the farmers. Contrast that result with a 180-degree shift in E.L. Doctorow's *Ragtime*, in which the disenfranchised form a family.

Summing Up

In Society Story, the Core Need for collective esteem and self-determination leads us to identify with the members of the disenfranchised class, and we respond to conflict on the power-impotence spectrum with intrigue, triumph or righteous indignation. In the Core Event, the Revolution scene, recognition is most in jeopardy, the life value of impotence is at the extreme, and the emotion of triumph or righteous indignation reaches its height, depending on whether the revolution succeeds or fails. By setting up and delivering this scene in an innovative way, you meet the Society genre reader's expectations.

13

STATUS STORY

Core Need: Respect
Core Life Value: Failure/Success
Core Emotion: Admiration or Pity
Core Event: The Big Choice

Status Story answers the complex question, "Will the luminary agent be able to rise in social standing and achieve society's definition of success, or will they discover and embrace their personal definition of success?" Status stories are about a luminary agent's quest to rise within their social group and what they're willing to do and sacrifice to achieve that.

Status stories further explore the individual's relationship with two hierarchies —the power/dominance hierarchy of haves and have nots found in all societies and the growth/cognition hierarchy of levels of learning found within our own minds. The

Status story's protagonist is actively negotiating an internal struggle between achieving a higher status in the world's power/dominance hierarchy and dedicating themselves exclusively to improving their skills and knowledge on the growth/cognition hierarchy.

How do you deliver the experience Status Story readers are looking for?

The ***Core Need for respect***, especially from outside oneself, arises when the inciting incident offers an opportunity or challenge related to the luminary agent's position in their arena.

The ***Core Life Value*** derived from the need for respect spans ***failure and success*** and gradations between and beyond. The negative end of the spectrum goes beyond failure to "selling out" and the positive end can include compromise on the way to success.

The Status genre includes four clear subgenres that depend on the luminary agent's strength of character and choices. The Pathetic subgenre features a weak protagonist who attempts to achieve success but fails, as in Thomas Hardy's *Tess of the D'Urbervilles.* The Tragic subgenre includes a hard-working protagonist whose mistakes doom them to failure, as in Theodore Dreiser's *American*

Tragedy. The Sentimental subgenre features a weak protagonist who nevertheless succeeds, as in Colm Tóibín's *Brooklyn.* And the popular Admiration subgenre features a strong, principled protagonist who refuses compromise and succeeds, as in Peter Maas's *Serpico* or the film *Gladiator.*

When the luminary agent stays true to their inner moral code and embraces their own definition of success rather than that of the external power structure, readers feel the ***Core Emotion*** of ***admiration,*** but if the luminary sells out or fails, we feel ***pity.***

The global crisis of Status Story brings us to the extreme edge of the failure-success spectrum as the luminary agent faces a dilemma about whether to risk failure while staying true to themselves or achieve sure success by choosing the power hierarchy. The risk of failure must be on the table in the ***Core Event,*** which is the ***Big Choice*** scene. The Big Choice, which is both the global climax and the climax of the Ending Payoff, integrates all three core essentials. The luminary agent's Core Need for respect defines the Core Life Value of success at stake, which when attained produces the Core Emotion of admiration, and when not attained produces pity.

Because Status stories are an internal genre, the nature of the Core Event is flavored by pairing of it with an external genre. A Status story paired with Performance will be different than a Status story paired with Crime.

The universal takeaway or controlling idea of a Status story is: *Staying true to one's own values, whether or not this leads to social betterment, defines success. But if one sells out—exchanging their values for meaningless rank, praise, or acquisitions—the result is failure.*

Status stories show us that we are the sum of our choices, and that our choices are substantially dictated by the external circumstances we face—opportunities, challenges, and the presence or absence of a mentor. These stories can often be read as a call for everyone to find a strong mentor and heed their advice as well as an invitation to *become* a strong mentor to others—providing the difference between a sentimental or tragic ending.

The Status genre speaks powerfully to writers, and creative "makers" of all kinds. A writer who never publishes a story because nothing they produce is "good enough" is an example of a luminary agent who has committed too much to the growth/cognition hierarchy. A writer who publishes first drafts without doing the necessary work to improve them and exploits technologies to profit from that work is an example of a luminary who veered too sharply toward the power/dominance hierarchy.

Find a mentor, and find another way that leads to self-respect, the respect of others, and success.

Summing Up

In Status stories, our need for respect from an external source allows us to identify with the luminary agent, and we respond to conflict on the failure-success spectrum with admiration when the luminary expresses their adherence to their own moral code in the Core Event of the Big Choice. Or we feel pity if they choose selling out and failure. During this event, the Core Need for respect is in jeopardy, the Core Emotion of admiration or pity reaches its height as a result of the luminary attaining their need, and the Life Value reaches an extreme. By setting up and delivering this scene in an innovative way, you meet the Status Story reader's expectations.

14

MORALITY STORY

Core Need: Self-Transcendence
Core Life Value: Selfishness/Altruism
Core Emotion: Satisfaction or Contempt
Core Event: The Big Choice

Morality Story answers the complex question, "When given a chance to behave selfishly or altruistically, which will we choose? Will we apply our unique gifts of knowledge, ability, and strength of will in service of darkness or light?" Morality stories are about making a choice to act on behalf of ourselves or others and the consequences of that choice. This choice is the culmination of a protagonist's journey from the bottom to the top of the hierarchy of human needs that began with Action Story.

How do you deliver the experience Morality Story readers are looking for?

The *Core Need for self-transcendence* arises after the inciting incident presents a shock to the hibernating self of the protagonist who has discovered and expressed their gifts in order to survive and thrive in the world. This is the moment when an opportunity presents itself for the luminary agent to contribute to the greater good and leave something of value in the world after their death.

The *Core Life Value* spectrum derived from the need for self-transcendence ranges from ***selfishness to altruism*** with several points in between involving sacrifice for the good of an individual, the family or tribe, or all of humanity.

When the luminary agent moves beyond selfish pursuits to express their gifts for the benefit of others, readers feel the *Core Emotion* of ***satisfaction***, perhaps because we feel inspired to express our gifts for others too. If the luminary withholds altruism and embraces selfishness, readers may feel contempt because the world and the protagonist have both lost an opportunity to experience transcendence.

Morality Story includes three subgenres: punitive, redemptive, and testing. The punitive story follows a protagonist who is also a villain.

They take a purely selfish path and are punished, as is the iconic Walter White in the *Breaking Bad* TV series or the title character in Henrik Ibsen's *Hedda Gabler*. The redemption story follows a character who is lost on the wrong path at the beginning but recognizes they have thrown away a great gift and reclaims that gift to redeem themselves and achieve altruism by the end, as in Nathaniel Hawthorne's *The Scarlet Letter*. In a testing story with a triumphant outcome, the protagonist struggles on a variety of paths, wavering before finding the right one that allows them to surrender to their purpose. The film *Forrest Gump* and the novel *For Whom the Bell Tolls* by Ernest Hemingway are examples of the testing subgenre. Sometimes characters are tested but can never escape the selfish path, surrendering to struggle and weakness, as in F. Scott Fitzgerald's *Tender is the Night*.

The universal takeaway or controlling idea of a morality story that is positive, or prescriptive, is: *We transcend our own selfishness when we share our gifts for the benefit of others.* The takeaway when the story ends negatively, or as a cautionary tale, is: *We are damned when we selfishly withhold our gifts or use them solely for our own gain in the world.* If we do succeed in transcending ourselves to leave a legacy of time well-spent on Earth, we will add the good we created to the collective unconscious of *Homo sapiens*.

Morality stories demonstrate that our actions define our character. It's important to note that morality stories are not about specific religious or philosophical systems of belief; they are about the search for meaning and purpose that allows us to contribute to the greater good. The luminary will have a revelation that lets them say, "I'm supposed to be doing this. I can move on and do my work in the way only I can do it." This is the "sweet spot" of being human. It is the moment when a writer or painter creates a timeless work of art that has its own magic to transcend, inspiring people in the present and future.

The global crisis of the Morality genre brings us to an extreme point on the selfishness-altruism spectrum as the luminary agent faces a dilemma about whether to express or withhold their gift in the ***Core Event,*** the ***Big Choice*** scene. The threat exists that the luminary will demonstrate selfish behavior. The Big Choice scene, which is both the global climax and the climax of the Ending Payoff, integrates all three core essentials. The luminary agent's Core Need for self-transcendence defines the Core Life Value of altruism at stake, which when attained produces a Core Emotion response of satisfaction in the reader.

While the luminary may make any number of selfish or altruistic choices throughout the story, it comes down to this single moment that will make all the difference. Their selfish or altruistic choice will determine the outcome for *others*, not just themselves.

Summing Up

In Morality Story, our need for self-transcendence allows us to identify with the luminary agent, and we respond to conflict on the selfishness-altruism spectrum with satisfaction or contempt, depending on the choice the luminary makes. In the Core Event, the Big Choice scene, transcendence is most in jeopardy, the Life Value reaches an extreme, and the Core Emotion reaches its height. By setting up and delivering this scene in an innovative way, you meet the Morality reader's expectations.

15

WORLDVIEW STORY

Core Need: Self-Actualization
Core Life Value: Ignorance/Wisdom
Core Emotion: Satisfaction or Pity
Core Event: Integral Cognitive Growth or Degeneration Event

Worldview Story answers the complex questions, "How can we solve problems we don't yet understand? How do we cope with events our existing belief structures cannot process?" These stories are about our perpetual human struggle to understand new information that contradicts the framework of our current knowledge and beliefs. A shake-up in our worldview is a threat to our very identity, but these stories are among the most powerful and inspiring for readers of both fiction and nonfiction.

How do you deliver the experience Worldview Story readers are looking for?

The Core Need to self-actualize arises when an inciting opportunity or challenge upsets the luminary agent's view of themselves or the world. The challenge starts to dismantle a portion of the luminary's current worldview, which allows for the creation of a new worldview and the actualization of their potential in the real world.

The *Core Life Value* of the Worldview genre derived from the need for self-actualization spans ***wisdom and ignorance,*** and gradations in between, including knowledge and cognitive dissonance. At the moment our core beliefs are challenged, we face cognitive dissonance, struggling to make sense of the world until we reach a moment of no return when we can't deny this new information any longer. It takes a cognitive leap to move from gathering new knowledge to acquiring the wisdom that constitutes a true worldview shift.

The four subgenres of Worldview depend on the specific kind of belief the luminary agent holds at the beginning of the story and how that transforms by the end. In the Disillusionment subgenre, the luminary begins with an unquestioned belief and ends with a loss of faith, as in F. Scott Fitzgerald's *The Great*

Gatsby. In the Education subgenre, the luminary evolves from a sense of meaninglessness to a sense of meaning, as in the musical, *My Fair Lady*. In the Maturation subgenre the luminary holds a rigid, black-and-white view of a particular aspect of the world, but by the end of the story has evolved to a more sophisticated "shades of gray" view, as in Harper Lee's *To Kill a Mockingbird*. Finally, in the Revelation subgenre, the luminary discovers the vital piece of missing information they need to make a wise decision, as in the film, *Arrival*.

When the luminary agent broadens and deepens their original worldview and attunes to the world, they attain the Core Life Value of wisdom. Readers feel the ***Core Emotion of satisfaction*** because if the luminary can become wise, perhaps we can too. If the luminary agent refuses to accept a new worldview after theirs has been shaken by the inciting challenge, we feel the ***Core Emotion of pity***. Not only the protagonist, but the world has lost a gift of insight that only that individual could provide.

The global crisis of Worldview forces the luminary agent to see and accept the world as it is and express their gifts or refuse. The ***Core Event***, or ***Cognitive Growth or Degeneration*** scene is one in which the luminary integrates challenging knowledge to produce a new worldview or refuses to integrate that information and allows their worldview to regress. Simply put, in this scene the luminary chooses to grow or regress. The Cognitive Growth or Degeneration scene, which is both the global climax and the climax of the Ending Payoff, integrates all three core essentials. The luminary's Core Need for self-actualization defines the Core Life Value of wisdom at stake, which—if attained—produces the Core Emotion response of satisfaction. If that Core Life Value of wisdom is not attained and ignorance reigns, the result is the Core Emotion response of pity.

Much of the action in a Worldview story happens in the luminary's mind, of course, so the Core Event is the writer's chance to demonstrate what the luminary does with the new knowledge or information that has challenged them. In the Core Event the protagonist actualizes or denies their new worldview.

The positive, cognitive growth version of the universal takeaway or controlling idea of a Worldview story is: *Wisdom and meaning prevail when we learn to express our gifts in a world we accept as imperfect.* The negative, degenerative version is: *Ignorance, naivete, and meaninglessness win when we fail to metabolize new information and release older, flawed beliefs to remake the way we see the world.*

Worldview stories show us that no matter how confident we are in our beliefs, we have more to learn. To self-actualize, we must improve our cognition by integrating old frames of reference into new, more accurate ones attuned to the natural world around us.

Summing Up

In worldview stories, our need for self-actualization allows us to identify with the protagonist. We respond to conflict on the ignorance-wisdom spectrum with the feeling of satisfaction when the luminary expresses their gifts and achieves cognitive growth and a worldview shift or feeling of pity when the luminary fails to achieve cognitive growth and degenerates instead. In the Core Event of cognitive growth or degeneration, the Core Need for self-actualization is most in jeopardy, the Life Value reaches an extreme, and the Core Emotions reach their height as a result of the luminary attaining their need. By setting up and delivering this scene in an innovative way, you meet Worldview Story reader's expectations.

THE FOUR CORE CONCLUSION

No writer sets out to write a story that doesn't resonate with and meet the expectations of readers of the genre, but it happens when we don't understand why readers go to a particular genre and what they expect to find.

Knowing the four core elements—need, life value, emotion, and event—for your chosen genre will help you provide readers with the emotional catharsis and knowledge they seek. When they face their own crises and core events, they will have a blueprint to consult for inspiration and support. When we see our beloved fictional characters rise, fall, and persist; when we see them win, lose, and grow more formidable in the process, we gain strength to survive the changes in our own lives.

Now it's time to use the Four Core

Framework as your own blueprint and support as you write your own story:

1. Decide what **Core Need** your protagonist and antagonist must fulfill.
2. Identify the **Core Life Value** associated with that particular need.
3. Describe the **Core Emotion** your audience should feel as they watch the main character's journey. If your readers don't feel anything, the story doesn't work.
4. Outline (or write out in a draft) the **Core Event** scene that brings together the Need, Life Value, and Emotion.

Write a story that will transform your readers' lives.

ABOUT THE AUTHOR

SHAWN COYNE created, developed, and expanded the story analysis and problem-solving methodology the Story Grid during his quarter-century-plus career in book publishing. A seasoned story editor, book publisher, and ghostwriter, Coyne has also co-authored *The Ones Who Hit the Hardest: The Steelers, the Cowboys, the '70s, and the Fight For America's Soul* with Chad Millman and *Cognitive Dominance: A Brain Surgeon's Quest to Out-Think Fear* with Mark McLaughlin, M.D. With his friend and editorial client Steven Pressfield, Coyne runs Black Irish Entertainment, LLC, publisher of the cult classic book *The War of Art.* Coyne oversees the Story Grid Universe, LLC, which includes Story Grid University and Story Grid Publishing, with his friend and editorial client Tim Grahl.

Made in the USA
Columbia, SC
26 November 2021